AQA GCSE ENGLISH LITERATURE PAPER 1 SECTION A: ROMEO AND JULIET: 12 A STAR EXAM PAPERS

Full mark A Star (Grade 9) Answers

By Joseph Anthony Campbell

CONTENTS

THE QUALITY CONTROL SYSTEM™ OR HOW TO GET AN A STAR!

The Quality Control System™ is fourfold.

It involves:

1) An efficient summary of the examination paper.

2) A concise focus upon the Assessment Objectives in the exam and how to approach them.

3) Clear instructions on your timings and how long you should spend on each question. This is the most important point of fact in this fourfold system.

4) Further to point 3, the approximate word count per mark you should be consistently aiming for in each minute of your exam.

My students have applied all of the techniques of the Quality Control System™ I am providing you with to gain A stars (Grade 9's) in their examinations. You can replicate them by following the advice in this book. Following these rules has ensured success for my students in English Literature and their other subjects and it will do for you too!

SUMMARY OF GCSE ENGLISH LITERATURE PAPER 1

This paper has a total of 64 marks.

There is 1 hour 45 minutes (105 minutes) for the exam (unless you have extra time).

Paper 1 is divided into 2 sections:

Paper 1 Section A: Shakespeare section. We are looking in this book at the **Romeo and Juliet option**. There are 12 examples of Grade 9, A star essays in this book. (I will be writing further books on alternative Shakespeare options).
Section A = 34 Marks (including 4 marks for spelling and grammar)

There will be one task on the Shakespeare play. You will respond to a short extract from the play and demonstrate your knowledge of the play as a whole.

Paper 1 Section B: Nineteenth Century Novel (I will be writing further books on options for this).
Section B = 30 Marks

The best approach is to spend 50 minutes on each question in Section A and B – 40 minutes writing and 10 minutes reading the extract, making notes and planning. Ideally leaving yourself 5 minutes for basic corrections and checking at the end of the examination.

ASSESSMENT OBJECTIVES

There are **four assessment objectives** assessed in each English Literature examination: **AO1, (12 Marks) AO2 (12 Marks) AO3 (6 Marks) and AO4 (4 marks for Spelling and Grammar) and AO4 is allocated ONLY in the Shakespeare section of Paper 1.**

AO1 = Read, understand and respond to text (Romeo and Juliet) and the task set in the question. Use 4 to 6 quotations from the text provided and ideally 2 to 3 short quotes you may have memorised from the rest of the play (or memorise those that I have provided in my answers in this book on various characters/themes in the play).

AO2 = Analyse the language, form and structure used by a writer (Shakespeare) to create meanings and effects i.e., also mention 'Shakespeare' 4 to 6 times in your answer and how he presents characters/themes and creates meanings and effects.

AO3 = is the understanding of the relationship between the ideas in the text and the context/time in which the text was written and the context within which the text is set.

AO4 = spell and punctuate with consistent accuracy, and consistently use vocabulary and sentence structures to achieve control of the meaning you are aiming to convey.

The Assessment Objectives are not provided in the examination itself. However, I have provided which assessment objectives are being assessed in the practice questions in this book. It is important to be aware of the structure of how the assessment objectives are allocated in each question of the exam in order to maximise your opportunities to obtain full marks in each question.

TIMINGS

In the English Literature GCSE Paper 1 examination there are 64 marks to aim for in 1 hour and 45 minutes (105 minutes). Please allocate the correct words per minute per mark! Again, to re-iterate: The best approach is to spend 50 minutes on each question in Section A and B - 40 minutes writing and 10 minutes reading the extract, making notes and planning. Ideally leaving yourself 5 minutes for basic corrections and checking at the end of the examination.

If you have extra time allocated to you, just change the calculation to accommodate the extra time you have i.e., if you have 25% extra time (= 50 minutes per question = 12 words per minute and 20 words per mark) and if you have 50% extra time (= 1 hour per question = 10 words per minute and 20 words per mark) also equals a 600-word essay for each section on Paper 1. Again, please allocate within your time management 5 minutes for checking at the end of the exam but please **move on from the set question as soon as you have reached or are coming towards your time limit**. This ensures that you have excellent coverage of your whole exam and therefore attain a very good mark.

Similar to all the principles in this book, **you must apply and follow the correct timings for each question and stick to them throughout your exam to get an A star (Grade 9) in your English Literature examinations.** Without applying this principle in these examinations (and to a large extent all examinations) you cannot achieve the highest marks! **Apply all of the principles provided in this book to succeed fully**!

APPROXIMATE WORD COUNT PER QUESTION IN ENGLISH LITERATURE PAPER 1

Now that you know what is on each examination, how the assessment objectives are assessed and the time allocated for each type of question; we come to what would be considered the correct word count per mark for each question. The primary principle though is to spend the right amount of time on each question.

In the answers in this book, I have provided the maximum word count for each answer which works out at **15 words per minute and 20 words per mark and therefore this equals a 600-word essay for each section on Paper 1**. If your answer has quality, this gives you the very best chance of obtaining the highest marks in your English Literature exam. Obviously, it does not if you are waffling however. (Please remember to answer the question set and to move on in the time allocated.)

I am aware that some students can write faster than others but all should be able to write 10 words per minute and thus a 400-word essay in the time (if they have not been allocated extra time). This is where conciseness is important in your writing.

My students and readers have applied all of the techniques of the Quality Control System™ I am providing you with; to gain A stars (Grade 9's) in their examinations. You can replicate them by following the advice in this book.

Thank you for purchasing this book and best wishes for your examinations! Joseph

ROMEO AND JULIET FIRST ESSAY – AGGRESSIVE MALE BEHAVIOUR

Read the following extract from Act 1 Scene 1 of <u>Romeo and Juliet</u> and then answer the question that follows.

At this point in the play, the male servants of the house of Capulet have seen the male servants from the house of Montague and a fight is about to start.

SAMPSON

My naked weapon is out. Quarrel, I will back thee.

GREGORY

How, turn thy back and run?

SAMPSON

Fear me not.

GREGORY

No, marry, I fear thee!

SAMPSON

5 Let us take the law of our sides, let them begin.

GREGORY

I will frown as I pass by, and let them take it as they list.

SAMPSON

Nay, as they dare. I will bite my thumb at them, which is disgrace to them if they bear it.

ABRAM

Do you bite your thumb at us, sir?

SAMPSON

10 I do bite my thumb, sir.

ABRAM

Do you bite your thumb at us, sir?

SAMPSON

[Aside to Gregory] Is the law of our side if I say ay?

GREGORY

[Aside to Sampson] No.

SAMPSON

No, sir, I do not bite my thumb at you, sir, but I bite my thumb, sir.

Starting with this conversation, explore how Shakespeare presents aggressive male behaviour in <u>Romeo and Juliet</u>.

Write about:

• *how Shakespeare presents aggressive male behaviour in this conversation*
• *how Shakespeare presents aggressive male behaviour in the play as a whole.*

[30 Marks] (AO1 = 12; AO2 = 12; AO3 = 6) + AO4 = Spelling and Grammar [4 marks]

(50 Minutes Total = 40 Minutes Writing + 10 Minutes Reading Extract / Making Notes / Planning)

(600 Words Maximum per Essay = 15 Words per Minute)

Shakespeare presents aggressive male behaviour in this conversation as Gregory and Sampson, both servants of the house of Capulet engage in conflict with members of the house of Montague. There is a tribal element to belonging to the house of Capulet or Montague and thus belonging to either family spurs conflict. Sampson states, "My naked weapon is out" using sexual imagery to represent and link a sense of masculinity to fighting. Although Gregory is initially hesitant to start a fight; he is prepared to begin the "Quarrel" with a "frown". Sampson, however, increases the levels of aggression through his decision to "...bite my thumb at them, which is disgrace to them if they bear it." Abram reacts to this perceived insult by asking Sampson directly, "Do you bite your thumb at us, sir?" with the use of the word "sir" implying mock civility. This sets in motion a situation whereby Abram (and later Balthasar) will defend their sense of perceived masculinity through aggressive actions and behaviour. Shakespeare also presents humour in this extract and to the conflict, through his use of stage directions as Sampson asks in an "[Aside to Gregory] Is the law of our side if I say ay?" and Gregory responds, "[Aside to Sampson] No." Overall, this conversation arguably presents stereotypical ideas as regards men and violence and as it is the opening scene in the play, Shakespeare is clearly presenting, in terms of the play's structure, a theme of aggressive male behaviour that will be prevalent throughout the play. The discussion and brawl presented in the opening scene exemplifies the rivalry, hatred and vicious cycle of violence between the Capulets and the Montagues; which pervades the rest of the play.

Shakespeare presents aggressive male behaviour in the play as a whole with a continuation of aggressive male behaviour throughout the play. Directly following this extract, as the Montagues retaliate to Capulet aggression, Benvolio arrives and aims to stop the fight, which signals the entrance of Tybalt. Sampson and Gregory are Tybalt's servants and Tybalt comes to their aid. Tybalt, a skilled swordsman; could be considered the play's principal antagonist and the personification of aggressive male behaviour. It is in Act 3, Scene 1 when Shakespeare's presentation of aggressive male behaviour and the severe repercussions of the bitter and violent feud between the Capulets and the Montagues reaches its crescendo. In this scene, Mercutio insults and instigates a fight with Tybalt, misguidedly defending what he perceives as Romeo's honour, and is subsequently killed by Tybalt and Romeo murders Tybalt in revenge. Before he dies, Mercutio casts "A plague o' both your houses!" pointing to what he believes is the root cause of his death; the hatred between the Capulets and Montagues. In Act 5, Scene 3 Romeo also kills Paris yet grants Paris' dying wish to be placed next to Juliet in the Capulet tomb. Aggressive male behaviour is here interspersed with a sense of honour.

Shakespeare's theme of aggressive male behaviour throughout the play is grounded in the context of a dominating male rivalry and a hatred that rules social relations. A feminist standpoint could argue that the tragic male experience in the play is equivalent to a sickness and that the blame for the family feud lies in Verona's patriarchal society and that its strict, masculine code of violence is the main force driving this tragedy. There would be clear contextual differences also in terms of potentially different audience reactions over time to this extract and the contemporary reception and view of the aggressive male behaviour contained both in this extract and throughout the play.

(600 words)

By Joseph Anthony Campbell

ROMEO AND JULIET SECOND ESSAY – PRINCE ESCALUS

Read the following extract from Act 1 Scene 1 of <u>Romeo and Juliet</u> and then answer the
question that follows.

At this point in the play Prince Escalus is intervening in a violent fracas between the
Capulets and the Montagues.

Prince Escalus

Rebellious subjects, enemies to peace,
Profaners of this neighbour-stained steel,--
Will they not hear? What, ho! you men, you beasts,
That quench the fire of your pernicious rage
5 With purple fountains issuing from your veins,
On pain of torture, from those bloody hands
Throw your mistemper'd weapons to the ground,
And hear the sentence of your moved prince.
Three civil brawls, bred of an airy word,
10 By thee, old Capulet, and Montague,
Have thrice disturb'd the quiet of our streets,
And made Verona's ancient citizens

Cast by their grave beseeming ornaments,

To wield old partisans, in hands as old,

15 Canker'd with peace, to part your canker'd hate:

If ever you disturb our streets again,

Your lives shall pay the forfeit of the peace.

For this time, all the rest depart away:

You Capulet; shall go along with me:

20 And, Montague, come you this afternoon,

To know our further pleasure in this case,

To old Free-town, our common judgment-place.

Once more, on pain of death, all men depart.

Starting with this speech, explore how Shakespeare presents Prince Escalus as an arbiter of justice and restoration in Romeo and Juliet.

Write about:

• *how Shakespeare presents Prince Escalus as an arbiter of justice and restoration in this speech*

• *how Shakespeare presents Prince Escalus as an arbiter of justice and restoration in the play as a whole*

[30 Marks] (AO1 = 12; AO2 = 12; AO3 = 6) + AO4 = Spelling and Grammar [4 marks]

(50 Minutes Total = 40 Minutes Writing + 10 Minutes Reading Extract / Making Notes / Planning)

(600 Words Maximum per Essay = 15 Words per Minute)

Shakespeare presents dramatic tension prior to this extract and, in this speech, presents Prince Escalus as an arbiter of justice through the use of the Prince's powerful rhetoric "...hear the sentence of your moved prince." We can discern that the

Prince has clearly been "moved" by the brawl and he proceeds to state facts through repeating the terminology of the "Three civil brawls" that "Have thrice disturb'd the quiet of our streets,". The Prince is clearly exasperated by these violent fracases as he asks a rhetorical question "Will they not hear?" and then clearly administers his judgement; "If ever you disturb our streets again, / Your lives shall pay the forfeit of the peace." Prince Escalus' Language highlights the power dynamic and his superior status to his citizens through his use of imperative, masculine language and his forceful phrasing which implies strength.

Shakespeare uses Prince Escalus as a principal character to influence the plot development. Prince Escalus is the Prince of Verona, and his reasons and motivation for this severe judgement is perhaps due to the fact that he is the desperate arbiter between these two feuding families. He is the voice of authority in Verona and he will punish Capulet and Montague for this violent quarrel. A theme and consideration of the play is: What is the just punishment for these two feuding families?

The Prince reinforces his decree at the end of the speech through the repetition of an emphatic statement and an imperative command, "Once more, on pain of death, all men depart." The structural significance of this moment in the play is a foreshadowing, as death will befall many before the plays end, through not heeding the Prince's decree stated here. The precision of the Prince's speech suggests that he is a concise man, enforcing his points with a brevity of words. Shakespeare's placing of the speech here, in terms of the plot's development, displays a structural theme of opposition that will continue throughout the play, between Prince Escalus and the feuding Capulet and Montague families.

Shakespeare presents Prince Escalus as an arbiter of justice and restoration throughout the rest of the play. He appears only two more times within the play, in Act 3 Scene 1 and at the play's conclusion in Act 5 Scene 3; whereby he administers justice after the tragic loss of lives. As the Prince observes his murdered kinsman Mercutio in Act 3 Scene 1, he states "I have an interest in your hate's proceeding, / My blood for your rude brawls doth lie a-bleeding". He also spares Romeo's life yet exiles him and declares "Mercy but murders, pardoning those that kill" as he believes pardoning killers fully will only cause more murders.

He is a clear arbiter of justice and Shakespeare exemplifies his desire for restoration also during the final scene of the play, as he demands answers despite Lord Montagues protestations, "Seal up the mouth of outrage for a while / Till we can clear these ambiguities,". His use of bold questions also highlights his powerful status. Surveying the tragic events that have resulted in the deaths of Lady Montague, Romeo, Juliet, and Tybalt he states that "Some shall be pardon'd, and some punished". When reflecting on his own loved ones; Mercutio and Paris, he states that he has "lost a brace of kinsmen: all are punish'd." The feud however now appears to have finally been resolved but at too great a price as demonstrated by the Prince's rhyming couplet that concludes the play: "For never was a story of more woe / Than this of Juliet and her Romeo."

(600 words)

ROMEO AND JULIET THIRD ESSAY – LORD CAPULET

Read the following extract from Act 1 Scene 2 of <u>Romeo and Juliet</u> and then answer the
question that follows.

At this point in the play Lord Capulet and Paris are discussing Juliet.

PARIS

But now, my lord, what say you to my suit?

CAPULET

But saying o'er what I have said before:
My child is yet a stranger in the world,
She hath not seen the change of fourteen years;
5 Let two more summers wither in their pride,
Ere we may think her ripe to be a bride.

PARIS

Younger than she are happy mothers made.

CAPULET

And too soon marred are those so early made.
The earth hath swallowed all my hopes but she;
10 She's the hopeful lady of my earth.
But woo her, gentle Paris, get her heart,
My will to her consent is but a part;
And she agreed, within her scope of choice
Lies my consent and fair according voice.

Starting with this conversation, explain how far you think Shakespeare presents Lord Capulet as a good father.

Write about:

• how Shakespeare presents Lord Capulet in this extract
• how Shakespeare presents Lord Capulet in the play as a whole.

[30 Marks] (AO1 = 12; AO2 = 12; AO3 = 6) + AO4 = Spelling and Grammar [4 marks]

(50 Minutes Total = 40 Minutes Writing + 10 Minutes Reading Extract / Making Notes / Planning)

(600 Words Maximum per Essay = 15 Words per Minute)

Lord Capulet's love for his daughter Juliet is clearly evidenced in the line, "The earth hath swallowed all my hopes but she;". Shakespeare also repeats this theme of how Juliet, Lord Capulet's only child, is his solitary 'hope' in the following line, "She's the hopeful lady of my earth." Lord Capulet's role is one of being a protector of his daughter and as Juliet's father, his chief role in Juliet's life is to be responsible for her marriage. He has raised and cared for Juliet for almost fourteen years, and he must find a suitable husband to continue to provide for her. His protective nature is outlined when he responds to Paris' marriage request with the lines, "But saying o'er what I have said before: /My child is yet a stranger in the world,". We can discern from the first line here that Lord Capulet has emphasised this point previously to Paris. There is a clear contrast between the length of Lord Capulet and Paris's speech also in this extract which implies Lord Capulet expects to both speak and to be heard which is further emphasised through Shakespeare's use of rhyming couplets. "Let two more summers wither in their pride, /Ere we may think her ripe to be a bride." Lord Capulet uses the imagery of the readiness of a harvest to emphasise Juliet's youth through the use of word choices such as 'wither' and 'ripe'.

Paris is persistent however and in terms of the society of the play and as regards marriage and its function during this time period, Paris would be considered a good match for Juliet. Count Paris is a kinsman of Prince Escalus and his wish is to make Juliet both his wife and the mother of his children. However, when Paris states, "Younger than she are happy mothers made" Capulet retorts and uses a repetition of the word 'made' in a protective and considered response in terms of his daughter's best interests, "And too soon marred are those so early made." Lord Capulet encourages Paris to "...woo her, gentle Paris, get her heart," and demonstrates the qualities of a good father who takes his child's view into consideration when he states. "My will to her consent is but a part;/ And she agreed...Lies my consent". Juliet has her own "choice" yet the viewpoint expressed by Lord Capulet here changes dramatically later in the play.

As the play abruptly shifts from a comedy to a tragedy and Juliet grieves over Romeo's departure, Capulet mistakenly assumes that her grief is due to Tybalt's death, and he hastily arranges a marriage between Juliet and Paris. This is in clear contrast to the "choice" Juliet previously had in Act 1, Scene 2. When Juliet refuses to become Paris' bride in Act 3 Scene 5, Capulet brands her a "hilding", calling her "unworthy", "young baggage" and a "disobedient wretch". The solitary hope that Juliet formerly represented is now defined by Lord Capulet as being, "...a curse".

However, in the play's final scene, when Juliet has died, it is in fact Lord Capulet who states, "O brother Montague, give me thy hand:", to finally end the bitter feud between their families; now realising fully that Juliet and Romeo are, "Poor sacrifices of our enmity!" Throughout the play, Lord Capulet is a protective, loving, considerate, commanding, harsh and finally, bitterly regretful, father. Ultimately, Lord Capulet as a dramatic character is not a human being with separate mental processes from those of Shakespeare and contemporary reception towards Lord Capulet would possibly contrast with a modern perception of Lord Capulet as a good father.

(600 words)

By Joseph Anthony Campbell

ROMEO AND JULIET FOURTH ESSAY – LADY CAPULET

Read the following extract from Act 1 Scene 3 of <u>Romeo and Juliet</u> and then answer the question that follows.

At this point in the play, Lady Capulet is speaking with Juliet in the presence of the Nurse.

LADY CAPULET

Verona's summer hath not such a flower.

Nurse

Nay, he's a flower; in faith, a very flower.

LADY CAPULET

What say you? can you love the gentleman?
This night you shall behold him at our feast;
5 Read o'er the volume of young Paris' face,
And find delight writ there with beauty's pen;
Examine every married lineament,
And see how one another lends content
And what obscured in this fair volume lies
10 Find written in the margent of his eyes.
This precious book of love, this unbound lover,
To beautify him, only lacks a cover:
The fish lives in the sea, and 'tis much pride

For fair without the fair within to hide:
15 That book in many's eyes doth share the glory,
That in gold clasps locks in the golden story;
So shall you share all that he doth possess,
By having him, making yourself no less.

Nurse

No less! nay, bigger; women grow by men.

LADY CAPULET

20 Speak briefly, can you like of Paris' love?

JULIET

I'll look to like, if looking liking move:
But no more deep will I endart mine eye
Than your consent gives strength to make it fly.

Starting with this conversation, explain how far you think Shakespeare presents Lady
Capulet as a good mother.

Write about:

• *how Shakespeare presents Lady Capulet as a good mother in this extract*
• *how Shakespeare presents Lady Capulet as a good mother in the play as a whole*

[30 Marks] (AO1 = 12; AO2 = 12; AO3 = 6) + AO4 = Spelling and Grammar [4 marks]

(50 Minutes Total = 40 Minutes Writing + 10 Minutes Reading Extract / Making Notes / Planning)

(600 Words Maximum per Essay = 15 Words per Minute)

There are contrasting viewpoints an audience could take as to whether Shakespeare presents Lady Capulet as a good mother in this extract and throughout the play as a whole. Earlier in the play, Lady Capulet reveals that she was a mother at a young age, "I was your mother much upon these years / that you are now a maid". In this extract, as Lady Capulet mentions Paris' proposal of marriage to Juliet, she employs a Petrarchan sonnet form to describe the qualities of Count Paris to Juliet. A Petrarchan sonnet has fourteen lines of poetry, divided into an eight-line subsection (octave) and a six-line subsection (sestet). Lady Capulet proceeds to use an extended literary metaphor and describes Paris as a handsome man "Read o'er the volume of young Paris' face, / And find delight writ there with beauty's pen" and compares Paris to a book, and Juliet as the cover. "This precious book of love ... only lacks a cover." The extended literary metaphor is further exemplified with the words, "story", "margent" (margin), "volume" and "written". The use of hyperbolic language and rhetoric used in this sonnet could suggest manipulation but also maternal care, in order to find her daughter, the most suitable match in marriage: "By having him, making yourself no less." There is a carefully ordered precision to Lady Capulet's speech and a clear alteration in tone when Lady Capulet uses an imperative command "Speak briefly," followed by a direct question "...can you like of Paris' love?" This one line highlights the power dynamic of matriarch and daughter which is similarly highlighted by the contrast between the length of Lady Capulet's speech and the three lines of Juliet in reply, "...no more deep will I endart mine eye/ Than your consent gives strength to make it fly." The use and effect of this concluding rhyming couplet demonstrates Juliet's subservience to her mother's command. There is a sense of ownership implied in Lady Capulet's imperative command and through this Juliet's lack of power is portrayed, at this moment in the play. Shakespeare's placing of this conversation early in the play suggests its key significance to the unfolding of the plot.

Lady Capulet's later attitude to Juliet's refusal to marry Paris in Act 3, Scene 5 provides a stark contrast, as she states to Capulet that, "I would the fool were married to her grave!" which provides an eerie foreshadowing of the later events of the play, when Lady Capulet will feel that she has lost her only daughter twice. Juliet's form of address is again respectful but distant as she appeals to "...my lady mother". However, Lady Capulet later states in the scene, "Talk not to me, for I'll not speak a word:/ Do as thou wilt, for I have done with thee." Lady Capulet delivers this speech in an eerie, emotionless manner as she coldly rejects and leaves her daughter. However, during the final Acts of the play, Lady Capulet is overcome by tragic events and the grief-stricken mother she is, is revealed in Act 4, Scene 5, "O me, O me! My child, my only life, / Revive, look up, or I will die with thee" and in Act 5, Scene 3 "O me! this sight of death is as a bell, / That warns my old age to a sepulchre."

Overall, there is a duality in Shakespeare's presentation of Lady Capulet and evidence both for and against her being a good mother. However, the roles of families and the rules of conformity to societal expectations for women in Shakespeare's time, contrasts greatly with modern expectations.

(600 words)

ROMEO AND JULIET FIFTH ESSAY – DIFFERING ATTITUDES TO LOVE OF ROMEO AND FRIAR LAURENCE

Read the following extract from Act 2 Scene 3 of <u>Romeo and Juliet</u> and then answer the
question that follows.

At this point in the play, Romeo has just asked the Friar to marry him and Juliet.

FRIAR LAURENCE

Be plain, good son, and homely in thy drift;
Riddling confession finds but riddling shrift.

ROMEO

Then plainly know my heart's dear love is set
On the fair daughter of rich Capulet:
5 As mine on hers, so hers is set on mine;
And all combined, save what thou must combine

By holy marriage: when and where and how
We met, we woo'd and made exchange of vow,
I'll tell thee as we pass; but this I pray,
10 That thou consent to marry us to-day.

FRIAR LAURENCE

Holy Saint Francis, what a change is here!
Is Rosaline, whom thou didst love so dear,
So soon forsaken? young men's love then lies
Not truly in their hearts, but in their eyes.
15 Jesu Maria, what a deal of brine
Hath wash'd thy sallow cheeks for Rosaline!
How much salt water thrown away in waste,
To season love, that of it doth not taste!
The sun not yet thy sighs from heaven clears,
20 Thy old groans ring yet in my ancient ears;
Lo, here upon thy cheek the stain doth sit
Of an old tear that is not wash'd off yet:
If e'er thou wast thyself and these woes thine,
Thou and these woes were all for Rosaline:
25 And art thou changed? pronounce this sentence then,
Women may fall, when there's no strength in men.

ROMEO

Thou chid'st me oft for loving Rosaline.

FRIAR LAURENCE

For doting, not for loving, pupil mine.

Starting with this conversation, explore how Shakespeare presents the differing attitudes to love of Romeo and Friar Laurence in ***Romeo and Juliet.***

Write about:

- *how Shakespeare presents the differing attitudes to love of Romeo and Friar Laurence in this conversation*
- *how Shakespeare presents the differing attitudes to love of Romeo and Friar Laurence in the play as a whole*

[30 Marks] (AO1 = 12; AO2 = 12; AO3 = 6) + AO4 = Spelling and Grammar [4 marks]

(50 Minutes Total = 40 Minutes Writing + 10 Minutes Reading Extract / Making Notes / Planning)

(600 Words Maximum per Essay = 15 Words per Minute)

Shakespeare presents the differing attitudes to love of Romeo and Friar Laurence in this conversation and it is presented by Shakespeare through rhyming couplets which provides a rhythmic and parallel structure to the wordplay. Romeo declares "Then plainly know my heart's dear love is set / On the fair daughter of rich Capulet:" and asks firmly of Friar Laurence and with great motivation, "That thou consent to marry us to-day". The Friar uses a metaphor with culinary imagery when he states; "How much salt water thrown away in waste, / To season love, that of it doth not taste!" This links to the theme of 'unrequited love' in his reply to Romeo's "Thou chid'st me oft for loving Rosaline" when he states, "For doting, not for loving, pupil mine." Romeo was only yesterday in love with Rosaline, which was unrequited and had no real substance and was instead merely "doting". The Friar's use of the word "pupil", his use of imperative language and rhetorical questions with a sarcastic tone, ("And art thou changed?") and the contrast between the length of the Friar's and Romeo's speeches in this extract highlight the power dynamic of teacher and student between the Friar and Romeo respectively. The Friar states that his attitude to the love of Romeo and all young men's love is that "...young men's love then lies / Not truly in their hearts, but in their eyes." And he finishes his point by stating, "Women may fall, when there's no strength in men." There is a duality and a seeming contradiction between both Romeo and Friar Laurence's different perceptions of love in this extract. There is also a structural significance to this moment of the play in terms of the narrative structure as Shakespeare sets the scene for the rest of the play. The placing of this conversation at an early stage of the play takes on key significance as the play progresses towards its tragic conclusion.

Shakespeare presents differing attitudes to love between Romeo and Friar Laurence in the play as a whole. At the beginning of the play, Romeo muses upon Rosaline in Act 1, Scene 1 and attempts to use the Petrarchan sonnet form. A Petrarchan sonnet has fourteen lines of poetry, divided into an eight-line subsection (an octave) and a six-line subsection (a sestet). Petrarchan sonnets were used to exemplify unrequited love through hyperbolic language, and this reflects Romeo's feelings for Rosaline at this point, "Feather of lead, bright smoke, cold fire, sick health! / Still-waking sleep, that is not what it is!" In Act 1, Scene 4, Romeo is still the classic and melodramatic, Petrarchan lover, as he states to Mercutio, "Is love a tender thing? it is too rough," to which Mercutio replies, "If love be rough with you, be rough with love;".

Romeo abandoning Rosaline for Juliet in Act 2 may be perceived as ungentlemanly, fickle and reckless. However, Shakespeare frequently uses sub-plots in his plays to offer a greater sense of clarity on a character and Romeo's infatuation with Rosaline is in clear contrast to the mutual love he has with Juliet and the audience can discern the true depth of feeling in Romeo and Juliet's love and marriage. Friar Laurence perhaps also notices this change in Romeo as he decides to marry him and Juliet in a vain attempt to end the bitter enmity between the Capulets and the Montagues. "For this alliance may so happy prove, / To turn your households' rancour to pure love." At this point of the play, Romeo and Friar Laurence's attitudes to love fully align and converge.

(600 words)

ROMEO AND JULIET SIXTH ESSAY – THE RELATIONSHIP BETWEEN THE NURSE AND JULIET

Read the following extract from Act 2 Scene 5 of <u>Romeo and Juliet</u> and then answer the
question that follows.

At this point in the play, Juliet awaits the Nurse, who has just arrived after giving Juliet's message to Romeo.

JULIET

I' faith, I am sorry that thou art not well.
Sweet, sweet, sweet nurse, tell me, what says my love?

Nurse

Your love says, like an honest gentleman, and a
courteous, and a kind, and a handsome, and, I
5 warrant, a virtuous,--Where is your mother?

JULIET

Where is my mother! why, she is within;
Where should she be? How oddly thou repliest!
'Your love says, like an honest gentleman,
Where is your mother?'

Nurse

10 O God's lady dear!
Are you so hot? marry, come up, I trow;
Is this the poultice for my aching bones?
Henceforward do your messages yourself.

JULIET

Here's such a coil! come, what says Romeo?

Nurse

15 Have you got leave to go to shrift to-day?

JULIET

I have.

Nurse

Then hie you hence to Friar Laurence' cell;
There stays a husband to make you a wife:
Now comes the wanton blood up in your cheeks,
20 They'll be in scarlet straight at any news.
Hie you to church; I must another way,
To fetch a ladder, by the which your love
Must climb a bird's nest soon when it is dark:
I am the drudge and toil in your delight,
25 But you shall bear the burden soon at night.
Go; I'll to dinner: hie you to the cell.

JULIET

Hie to high fortune! Honest nurse, farewell

Starting with this moment in the play, explore how Shakespeare presents the relationship between the Nurse and Juliet in <u>*Romeo and Juliet.*</u>

Write about:

• *How the relationship between the Nurse and Juliet is presented at this moment in the play*

- *How the relationship between the Nurse and Juliet is presented in the play as a whole*

[30 Marks] (AO1 = 12; AO2 = 12; AO3 = 6) + AO4 = Spelling and Grammar [4 marks]

(50 Minutes Total = 40 Minutes Writing + 10 Minutes Reading Extract / Making Notes / Planning)

(600 Words Maximum per Essay = 15 Words per Minute)

Shakespeare presents the relationship between the Nurse and Juliet at this moment in the play as having a gentle dynamic with a playful aspect that is shared between two confidantes, as the Nurse's question to Juliet and her use of imagery reflects, "Is this the poultice for my aching bones? /Henceforward do your messages yourself". The Nurse willingly acts as a messenger for Juliet and demonstrates that she cares deeply about Juliet's happiness. It could be posited that Juliet deftly uses the loyalties of the Nurse for her own advantage, and to an extent manipulates the Nurse, however, it is clear that the Nurse is a willing partner in this role, and is thus complicit in the outcome through which a new and heightened intimacy is revealed between the Nurse and Juliet in this extract. This is reflected in the Nurse's statement that, "I am the drudge and toil in your delight," and her delivery of the news that Juliet has eagerly awaited, "Then hie you hence to Friar Laurence' cell; /There stays a husband to make you a wife:" The Nurse's approval is also of deep importance to Juliet as reflected by her delight and her use of the word, "Honest" to describe the Nurse, "Hie to high fortune! Honest nurse, farewell". There is a discernible difference between the length of the Nurse's speech and Juliet's and the precision of Juliet's speech and her exclamatory remarks reflect the urgency in both her speech and her actions. There is also a clear contrast between the beginning of the extract and the tension Juliet feels through the Nurse's playful teasing and Juliet's delight and resolution at the conclusion of the extract.

Shakespeare presents the relationship between the Nurse and Juliet throughout the play with the Nurse as Juliet's servant, guardian and former wet nurse as shown when she states in Act 1 Scene 3, "...were not I thine only nurse, I would say thou hadst suck'd wisdom from thy teat." The Nurse is Juliet's foremost confidante and Juliet is to her a surrogate daughter. The Nurse and Juliet's relationship remains pivotal to the plot's development but continues to change in accordance with the development of the changing situations and dynamics throughout the play. Their relationship progressively transitions from a relatively straight-forward relationship to a much more complex dynamic.

The abrupt shift of the tone of the play from comedy to tragedy begins with Tybalt's death at the hands of Romeo as the Nurse proclaims, "He's dead, he's dead, he's dead! We are undone, lady,". In Act 3 Scene 5, Lord Capulet's threatening and bullying behaviour when Juliet refuses to marry Paris results in the Nurse aiming to perhaps protect both herself and Juliet, and thus advising Juliet (now secretly wed to Romeo) to effectively commit bigamy. This reveals a significant change in the relationship between the Nurse and Juliet. Juliet experiences this as the ultimate betrayal and it is this quintessential moment that severs her relationship with the Nurse as she emotionally isolates herself from the Nurse and dismisses her former confidante with the line "...thou hast comforted me marvellous much. Go in:"

In Act 4 Scene 5, the Nurse discovers Juliet under the influence of Friar Laurence's potion and this is the final moment of their relationship. However, Shakespeare also presents them as bravely undermining the hatred between the Capulets and the Montagues and aiming to forge a more harmonious future earlier in the play. Shakespeare's presentation of the relationship between the Nurse and Juliet reflects both its structural significance and central importance to the dramatic context of the play.

(600 words)

ROMEO AND JULIET SEVENTH ESSAY – MERCUTIO

Read the following extract from Act 3 Scene 1 of <u>Romeo and Juliet</u> and then answer the
question that follows.

At this point in the play Mercutio has been gravely wounded by Tybalt.

MERCUTIO

I am hurt.
A plague o' both your houses! I am sped.
Is he gone, and hath nothing?

BENVOLIO

What, art thou hurt?

MERCUTIO

5 Ay, ay, a scratch, a scratch; marry, 'tis enough.
Where is my page? Go, villain, fetch a surgeon.

Exit Page

ROMEO

Courage, man; the hurt cannot be much.

MERCUTIO

No, 'tis not so deep as a well, nor so wide as a
church-door; but 'tis enough,'twill serve: ask for
10 me to-morrow, and you shall find me a grave man. I
am peppered, I warrant, for this world. A plague o'
both your houses! 'Zounds, a dog, a rat, a mouse, a
cat, to scratch a man to death! a braggart, a
rogue, a villain, that fights by the book of
15 arithmetic! Why the devil came you between us? I
was hurt under your arm.

ROMEO

I thought all for the best.

MERCUTIO

Help me into some house, Benvolio,
Or I shall faint. A plague o' both your houses!
20 They have made worms' meat of me: I have it,
And soundly too: your houses!

Starting with this moment in the play, explore how Shakespeare presents Mercutio in Romeo and Juliet.

Write about:

- *How Mercutio is presented at this moment in the play.*
- *How Mercutio is presented in the play as a whole.*

[30 Marks] (AO1 = 12; AO2 = 12; AO3 = 6) + AO4 = Spelling and Grammar [4 marks]

(50 Minutes Total = 40 Minutes Writing + 10 Minutes Reading Extract / Making Notes / Planning)

(600 Words Maximum per Essay = 15 Words per Minute)

Mercutio is presented by Shakespeare in this extract, moments before his death at Tybalt's hands. Mercutio uses an extended metaphor of Tybalt as the "prince of cats", stating, "Ay, ay, a scratch, a scratch; marry, 'tis enough." And exclaims, "Zounds, a dog, a rat, a mouse, a / cat, to scratch a man to death!" ("Zounds" was a strong swear word in Shakespeare's time, referring to Christ's wounds that he suffered on the cross.) Before he dies, Mercutio makes one final pun declaring "...ask for me to-morrow, and you shall find me a grave man" a fearful image which corresponds with his later line, "They have made worms' meat of me:" His dire situation contrasts heavily with his keen humour and the comic references that he upholds until the end of his life. As Mercutio faces his impending death, he asks Romeo with incredulity "Why the devil came you between us? I / was hurt under your arm." This question changes the dynamic of Mercutio's words and reflects his vulnerability. He also uses a triplet, by stating "A plague o' both your houses!" three times in this extract and his final words are "your houses!" His use of exclamatory remarks, emphatic statements and repetition reinforce his feelings of acute indignance and dismay at the Capulet and Montague feud which he holds entirely responsible for his untimely demise. Mercutio's use of imperative, masculine language and forceful hyperbole in his phrasing, implies strength but masks a lack of strength (literally). Shakespeare' skilful presentation of the dramatic nature of this moment in the play presents us with the dramatic irony of Mercutio projecting an indignant and fiery protestation whilst he is inexorably losing his life. Shakespeare ultimately uses Mercutio's death to represent the dysfunction of the bitter feud between the Capulets and the Montagues and its devastating effect on the youth of Verona.

Mercutio is a highly effective character throughout the play and Shakespeare's presentation of his death is a structurally significant moment in the play and dramatically displays the theme of opposition between "both...houses" of Capulet and Montague. Mercutio is a pivotal character and his death has vast implications as prior to Mercutio's death, the play is largely a comedy and after his demise, the play suddenly becomes a tragedy and the genre and tone of the play change markedly. In terms of the dramatic context – this spectacle of fierce dramatic tension would be appreciated by an audience during Shakespeare's time.

Mercutio is presented in the play as a whole by Shakespeare as the cousin of Prince Escalus and Count Paris, and he is a close friend of Romeo and his cousin Benvolio. He performs a rhapsody in Act 1 Scene 4 with his Queen Mab speech, beginning with the lines, "I see Queen Mab hath been with you. / She is the fairies' midwife" which demonstrates his wit and his jesting, free spirited nature and flamboyant personality. Mercutio's sense of humour can also at times be facetious or even coarse and laden with innuendo and he may also be perceived as ungentlemanly, as when in Act 2 Scene 4 he exclaims "A sail! A sail!" to imply the Nurse is as big as a ship and refers to her as an "ancient lady". He is also impulsive and reckless and he can have a mean-spirited humour, declaring falsely to Benvolio in Act 3, Scene 1 that Benvolio is, "...as soon moved to be moody, and as soon moody to be moved." Shakespeare ultimately presents him as prone to moodiness and sudden outbursts of temper, which leads to his untimely demise.

(599 words)

ROMEO AND JULIET EIGHTH ESSAY – FRIAR LAURENCE

Read the following extract from Act 3 Scene 3 of <u>Romeo and Juliet</u> and then answer the
question that follows.

At this point in the play, Friar Laurence consoles Romeo by illustrating his blessings and providing him with hope for his future.

Friar Laurence

What, rouse thee, man! thy Juliet is alive,
For whose dear sake thou wast but lately dead;
There art thou happy: Tybalt would kill thee,
But thou slew'st Tybalt; there are thou happy too:
5 The law that threaten'd death becomes thy friend
And turns it to exile; there art thou happy:
A pack of blessings lights up upon thy back;
Happiness courts thee in her best array;
But, like a misbehaved and sullen wench,
10 Thou pout'st upon thy fortune and thy love:
Take heed, take heed, for such die miserable.
Go, get thee to thy love, as was decreed,
Ascend her chamber, hence and comfort her:
But look thou stay not till the watch be set,
15 For then thou canst not pass to Mantua;
Where thou shalt live, till we can find a time
To blaze your marriage, reconcile your friends,

Beg pardon of the prince, and call thee back
With twenty hundred thousand times more joy
20 Than thou went'st forth in lamentation.
Go before, nurse: commend me to thy lady;
And bid her hasten all the house to bed,
Which heavy sorrow makes them apt unto:
Romeo is coming.

Explore how far Shakespeare presents Friar Laurence as an advisor to Romeo in Romeo and Juliet.

Write about:

• *how Shakespeare presents Friar Laurence as an advisor to Romeo at this moment in the play.*
• *how Shakespeare presents Friar Laurence as an advisor to Romeo in the play as a whole.*

[30 Marks] (AO1 = 12; AO2 = 12; AO3 = 6) + AO4 = Spelling and Grammar [4 marks]

(50 Minutes Total = 40 Minutes Writing + 10 Minutes Reading Extract / Making Notes / Planning)

(600 Words Maximum per Essay = 15 Words per Minute)

Friar Laurence plays the part of an advisor through mentoring Romeo, and is pivotal in major plot developments. Shakespeare presents Friar Laurence in this extract as a forceful advisor as he bluntly states to Romeo, "What, rouse thee, man! thy Juliet is alive,". His use of imperative language here highlights the relationship and the power dynamic between Friar Laurence and his advisee Romeo. His use of rhetoric and masculine language and forceful phrasing here imply strength and influence over Romeo. The Friar's strong words and attitude towards Romeo may defy societal expectations but there are reasons and motivation for the Friar's reactions. He proves himself in this extract to be an effective character in the play as he proceeds to console Romeo by illustrating his blessings with the triplet "there art thou happy" which through repetition conveys dramatic and rhetorical irony through the use and effect of these particular words and the parallel structure of the wordplay. His repeated use of contrast and his use of emphatic statements heighten and emphasise Romeo's blessings which are in seeming and direct contradiction to how Romeo himself perceives these events. Although the Friar could be perceived as ungentlemanly and manipulative here. He states, "A pack of blessings lights up upon thy back; / Happiness courts thee in her best array;". He then provides Romeo with hope for his future, "...and call thee back / With twenty hundred thousand times more joy ...Romeo is coming." There is a clear and marked contrast between the beginning and the conclusion of this extract and a clear duality in tone as the Friar begins forcefully advising Romeo then rousing him with the foretelling of joyful events to come. Shakespeare uses this speech in the play to influence the plots development and the Friar is a pivotal character that drives the plot and the dramatic nature of this moment in the play has clear structural significance. The Friar also potentially endears himself to the audience through this speech.

At the end of the balcony scene of Act 2 Scene 2 Romeo states "Hence will I to my ghostly father's cell, His help to crave,". Romeo urgently requires the "help" of his advisor and his spiritual ("ghostly") father. It is therefore clear that Shakespeare presents Friar Laurence as the principal advisor to Romeo throughout the play. When we are first introduced to the character of the Friar in Act 2 Scene 3 by Shakespeare, his soliloquy regarding plants, uses the imagery of nature, to relate the plants similarities to humans and foreshadows the events of the play to come. In choosing forms, Shakespeare matches poetic form to character. Friar Laurence, for example, uses sermon and sententiae forms. When Romeo requests later in this scene that the Friar marry him to Juliet, he is initially taken aback due to Romeo's former unrequited infatuation with Rosaline but later agrees to marry them in order to forge a loving alliance between the Capulets and the Montagues. Yet at the conclusion of this scene Friar Laurence uses a sententia, "Wisely and slow; they stumble that run fast" which mirrors a central theme of the play; haste. Tragically, Romeo's impulsiveness, deriving from his haste and despite the wise counsel of his "ghostly father, indirectly leads to both Mercutio's death and to the double suicide of this newly married couple.

As the play progresses, different perceptions of the Friar come to light for the audience
and the dramatic context and spectacle he provides as an advisor and a pivotal driving force in the plot would have been largely appreciated by an audience during Shakespeare's time.

(600 words)

ROMEO AND JULIET NINTH ESSAY – RELATIONSHIPS BETWEEN ADULTS AND YOUNG PEOPLE

Read the following extract from Act 3 Scene 5 of <u>Romeo and Juliet</u> and then answer the
question that follows.

At this point in the play, Juliet has just been told that she must marry Paris.

CAPULET

How now, wife,
Have you delivered to her our decree?

LADY CAPULET

Ay, sir, but she will none, she gives you thanks.
I would the fool were married to her grave.

CAPULET

5 Soft, take me with you, take me with you, wife.
How, will she none? doth she not give us thanks?
Is she not proud? doth she not count her blest,
Unworthy as she is, that we have wrought
So worthy a gentleman to be her bride?

JULIET

10 Not proud you have, but thankful that you have:
Proud can I never be of what I hate,
But thankful even for hate that is meant love.

CAPULET

How now, how now, chopt-logic? What is this?
'Proud', and 'I thank you', and 'I thank you not',
15 And yet 'not proud', mistress minion you?
Thank me no thankings, nor proud me no prouds,
But fettle your fine joints 'gainst Thursday next,
To go with Paris to Saint Peter's Church,
Or I will drag thee on a hurdle thither.
20 Out, you green-sickness carrion! out, you baggage!
You tallow-face!

Starting with this moment in the play, explore how Shakespeare presents relationships between adults and young people in Romeo and Juliet.

Write about:

• *how Shakespeare presents relationships between adults and young people at this moment in the play*
• *how Shakespeare presents relationships between adults and young people in the play as a whole.*

[30 Marks] (AO1 = 12; AO2 = 12; AO3 = 6) + AO4 = Spelling and Grammar [4 marks]

(50 Minutes Total = 40 Minutes Writing + 10 Minutes Reading Extract / Making Notes / Planning)

(600 Words Maximum per Essay = 15 Words per Minute)

Shakespeare presents relationships between adults and young people at this moment in the play as Lord Capulet enquires of Lady Capulet, "Have you delivered to her (Juliet) our decree?" to which Lady Capulet responds, "I would the fool were married to her grave". This proves to be an eerie foreshadowing of the later events of the play and is similar in tone to Lady Capulet's response later in this scene when Juliet appeals for her mother's aid, "Talk not to me, for I'll not speak a word: /Do as thou wilt, for I have done with thee" which is stated in a cold, emotionless manner. In this extract, Juliet refuses her father's attempt to force her to marry Count Paris and through this action, she is challenging the patriarchal order of the time in which there is no consideration of her wishes. Lord Capulet is shocked by Juliet's refusal, viewing his daughter as a marriageable commodity, "How now, how now, chopt-logic? What is this?" Both he and Lady Capulet are entirely unaware of the fact that Juliet has just bid farewell to her husband Romeo and that Capulet's hastily declared arranged marriage places Juliet in an impossible position. There is also a sense of dramatic irony in terms of the profound secrets that exist between Juliet and her parents at this moment in the play. An emotionally violent scene ensues between Juliet and Lord Capulet, with Lord Capulet being verbally abusive and threatening to be physically abusive. There is a clear contrast between Juliet's language and Lord Capulet's language as Juliet thoughtfully and with consideration states, "Not proud you have, but thankful that you have:" Despite Juliet's attempt at reason, Capulet aggressively mimics Juliet stating, "'Proud', and 'I thank you', and 'I thank you not', /And yet 'not proud'". Lord Capulet's use of imperative language highlights the dynamic of powerful parent and powerless child that exists between him and his daughter at this moment in the play. He uses insulting language, proclaiming Juliet as "unworthy", and a "green-sickness carrion" yet there would be clear contextual differences in terms of potentially different audience reactions over time to this extract and the social structures that were in place during the time period this play is set in.

Shakespeare presents relationships between adults and young people throughout the play and provides a contrast through the Montague family's parental care of Romeo. Lord Montague clearly loves his son deeply and at the beginning of the play, he is worried about him and after Romeo kills Tybalt, he also pleads with the Prince to spare Romeo's life. Lady Montague is also very protective of her son Romeo and is extremely happy when he is not involved in the brawl at the beginning of the play. Whilst Lady Capulet defines Juliet as her property and a servant to her will, the Nurse is the primary person who raised Juliet and is her trusted confidante. However, the Nurse's advice to Juliet to marry Paris has a terminally destructive impact upon their relationship. In a parallel role to the Nurse, Friar Laurence is a confidant and parental figure to Romeo and plays the part of an advisor and mentor. Friar Laurence marries Romeo and Juliet in an attempt to end the bitter feud between the Capulets and the Montagues and when Romeo is banished, he tries to help them reunite using a death-emulating potion to fake Juliet's death. However, this cannot prevent Romeo and Juliet's tragic deaths and at the end of the play it is Lord Capulet who recognises that they are "Poor sacrifices of our enmity!"

(600 words)

ROMEO AND JULIET TENTH ESSAY – JULIET

Read the following extract from Act 4 Scene 3 of <u>Romeo and Juliet</u> and then answer the
question that follows.

At this point in the play, Juliet is about to drink the vial that Friar Laurence has given
her to give her the appearance of death.

JULIET

Shall I not, then, be stifled in the vault,
To whose foul mouth no healthsome air breathes in,
And there die strangled ere my Romeo comes?
Or, if I live, is it not very like,
5 The horrible conceit of death and night,
Together with the terror of the place,--
As in a vault, an ancient receptacle,
Where, for these many hundred years, the bones
Of all my buried ancestors are packed:
10 Where bloody Tybalt, yet but green in earth,
Lies festering in his shroud; where, as they say,
At some hours in the night spirits resort;--
Alack, alack, is it not like that I,

So early waking, what with loathsome smells,
15 And shrieks like mandrakes' torn out of the earth,
That living mortals, hearing them, run mad:--
O, if I wake, shall I not be distraught,
Environed with all these hideous fears?
And madly play with my forefather's joints?
20 And pluck the mangled Tybalt from his shroud?
And, in this rage, with some great kinsman's bone,
As with a club, dash out my desperate brains?
O, look! methinks I see my cousin's ghost
Seeking out Romeo, that did spit his body
25 Upon a rapier's point: stay, Tybalt, stay!
Romeo, I come! this do I drink to thee.

[She falls upon her bed, within the curtains]

Explore how far Shakespeare presents Juliet as a character who is determined in Romeo and Juliet.

Write about:

• *how Shakespeare presents Juliet as a character who is determined at this moment in the play.*
• *how Shakespeare presents Juliet as a character who is determined in the play as a whole.*

[30 Marks] (AO1 = 12; AO2 = 12; AO3 = 6) + AO4 = Spelling and Grammar [4 marks]

(50 Minutes Total = 40 Minutes Writing + 10 Minutes Reading Extract / Making Notes / Planning)

(600 Words Maximum per Essay = 15 Words per Minute)

Shakespeare presents Juliet as a character who is evidently determined at this moment in the play. The language used in the extract suggests how fearful Juliet understandably is of what will happen once she drinks the vial and is placed in her family tomb, "Where, for these many hundred years, the bones/ Of all my buried ancestors are packed:" Her determination is heavily tested by her fears as she considers the implications of what may occur, such as death "And there die strangled ere my Romeo comes?", intense fear "O, if I wake, shall I not be distraught,/ Environed with all these hideous fears?" and insanity "And madly play with my forefather's joints?/ And pluck the mangled Tybalt from his shroud?" Her use of these examples and her repetition of these fearful questions reinforce, heighten and emphasise the disordered state of her mind throughout this soliloquy. This is demonstrated also through her use of fearful images and hyperbolic language.

As the soliloquy develops Juliet perhaps hallucinates as she states, "O, look! methinks I see my cousin's ghost/ Seeking out Romeo" and clearly delineates that her loyalties lie with her husband rather than her cousin as she proclaims, "stay, Tybalt, stay! / Romeo, I come! this do I drink to thee." Shakespeare's use of imperative commands, exclamatory remarks and emphatic statements here, alongside Juliet's hyperbolic, forceful phrasing and her use of masculine language demonstrates Juliet's strength and determination. Her determined nature is exemplified in the stage direction that follows as, "[She falls upon her bed...] after drinking from the vial. Her clear sense of determination at the end of the extract contrasts with her doubts and fears that are prevalent throughout the remainder of the extract. There has been an increase of dramatic tension prior to this moment in the play and Shakespeare uses Juliet's soliloquy to influence the development of the plot and it is of vital structural importance to the narrative. Although it could be debated that Juliet submits to a female code of docility by allowing the Friar to attempt to solve her problems, she also endears herself to the audience through her sense of determination in this soliloquy which adds intense tension and power to this scene, in a clearly dramatic moment of the play.

Shakespeare presents Juliet as a character who is determined in this extract but also in other scenes. Juliet Capulet is the only child of the Capulet house who falls in love with Romeo, a Montague, with whom the Capulets have a bitter feud. During the balcony scene in Act 2, Scene 2, Juliet bluntly asks Romeo "Dost thou love me?" and consents to be married after only one night, which again illustrates her determined nature. Juliet demonstrates honour as she performs an epithalamium (a poem celebrating marriage) in Act 3 Scene 2 before her wedding night, "He will make the face of heaven so fine/ That all the world will be in love with night". When the Nurse advises Juliet to effectively commit bigamy in Act 3 Scene 5, Juliet experiences this as an intense betrayal and it is this quintessential moment that severs her relationship with the Nurse as she states "...thou hast comforted me marvellous much. / Go in". Juliet's clear ideas as regards honour and marriage could be viewed as unusual in a young woman. This also reflects her determined nature. Shakespeare most exemplifies Juliet as a character who is determined in Act 5 Scene 3 when she grabs Romeo's dagger, stating "O happy dagger! This is thy sheath. There rust, and let me die." And thus, commits suicide.

(600 words)

ROMEO AND JULIET ELEVENTH ESSAY – PARIS

Read the following extract from Act 5 Scene 3 of _Romeo and Juliet_ and then answer the
question that follows.

At this point in the play, Paris is in the churchyard visiting Juliet's tomb.

PARIS

Give me thy torch, boy: hence, and stand aloof:
Yet put it out, for I would not be seen.
Under yond yew-trees lay thee all along,
Holding thine ear close to the hollow ground;
5 So shall no foot upon the churchyard tread,
Being loose, unfirm, with digging up of graves,
But thou shalt hear it: whistle then to me,
As signal that thou hear'st something approach.
Give me those flowers. Do as I bid thee, go.

PAGE

10 [Aside] I am almost afraid to stand alone
Here in the churchyard; yet I will adventure.

Retires

PARIS

Sweet flower, with flowers thy bridal bed I strew,--
O woe! thy canopy is dust and stones;--
Which with sweet water nightly I will dew,
15 Or, wanting that, with tears distill'd by moans:
The obsequies that I for thee will keep
Nightly shall be to strew thy grave and weep.

[The Page whistles]

The boy gives warning something doth approach.
What cursed foot wanders this way to-night,
20 To cross my obsequies and true love's rite?
What with a torch! muffle me, night, awhile.

[Retires]

Starting with this moment in the play, explore how Shakespeare presents the character of Paris in _Romeo and Juliet_.

Write about:

- *How Paris is presented at this moment in the play.*
- *How Paris is presented in the play as a whole.*

[30 Marks] (AO1 = 12; AO2 = 12; AO3 = 6) + AO4 = Spelling and Grammar [4 marks]

(50 Minutes Total = 40 Minutes Writing + 10 Minutes Reading Extract / Making Notes / Planning)

(600 Words Maximum per Essay = 15 Words per Minute)

Paris is presented at this moment during his final appearance in the final scene of the play, as his Page accompanies him to the Capulet crypt whilst he mourns Juliet. He is dually worried that he will be disturbed or that someone may attempt to desecrate Juliet's tomb and states to the Page that the ground, "Being loose, unfirm, with digging up of graves, /...thou shalt hear it." The Page who stands guard is ordered by Paris to "...whistle then to me, /As signal that thou hear'st something approach" and Paris then dismisses him, "Give me those flowers. Do as I bid thee, go". Although Paris's language highlights the power dynamic between them, the lack of imperative language may imply that he gently commands him. Shakespeare presents the misgivings of the Page through stage directions and the lines, "[Aside] I am almost afraid to stand alone/ Here in the churchyard;". This ominous foreboding foreshadows the events of the play that are soon to transpire.

Paris has visited the crypt to quietly and privately mourn the loss of his fiancée. Paris wishes to mourn her in solitude and privacy. He professes his love to Juliet, through an elegy, saying he will nightly weep for her using elegiac language, "Which with sweet water nightly I will dew," and "...with tears distill'd by moans:". There is a repetition of the word "Nightly" which emphasises his devotion to Juliet in the last line of his elegy, "Nightly shall be to strew thy grave and weep." There is a sense of honourable intention when Paris states, "The obsequies that I for thee will keep". "Obsequies" means funeral rites, and the word is repeated by Shakespeare once again when the Page warns Paris that someone approaches. Paris wonders who has come "To cross my obsequies and true love's rite?" This question demonstrates a change in the dynamic.

Shakespeare presents Paris as an effective character in the play and a skilful orator through his use of rhetoric in this elegy. There is a clear duality presented by Shakespeare between Paris' loyalty to Juliet and his complete unawareness of Juliet's lack of feeling for him; which demonstrates dramatic irony. There is a precision and arguably a lack of spontaneity in Paris' speech as he performs his "obsequies" yet his sense of honour and loyalty potentially endear him to an audience. Shakespeare has thus far presented a dramatic build-up of tension prior to this extract and uses the character of Paris to influence the plot's development and set the scene through this structurally significant moment of the play.

Shakespeare presents Paris throughout the play as the kinsman of Prince Escalus who seeks to make Juliet his wife and the mother of his children. Count Paris would have been considered an appropriate match for Juliet and arranged marriages were common for aristocrats of a higher social order. In Act 4 Scene 1 Paris states, "Juliet, on Thursday early will I rouse ye:/ Till then, adieu; and keep this holy kiss." This could present an idea of ownership on Paris' behalf rather than love.

In his last appearance, Paris approaches Romeo (who is deranged by grief himself) to "...apprehend thee for a felon here". In the ensuing duel Paris is killed, and his dying wish is for Romeo to lay him next to Juliet, "O, I am slain! /If thou be merciful, /Open the tomb, lay me with Juliet." Romeo does this, laying him beside Juliet's body and thus fulfilling Paris's dying wish and the dramatic context of this action would have been fully appreciated by an audience during Shakespeare's time.

(600 words)

ROMEO AND JULIET TWELFTH ESSAY – ROMEO

Read the following extract from Act 5 Scene 3 of <u>Romeo and Juliet</u> and then answer the
question that follows.

At this point in the play, Romeo is looking upon Juliet, whom he believes to be dead,
as she lays in a tomb belonging to the Capulets.

Romeo

Ah, dear Juliet,
Why art thou yet so fair? shall I believe
That unsubstantial death is amorous,
And that the lean abhorred monster keeps
5 Thee here in dark to be his paramour?
For fear of that, I still will stay with thee;
And never from this palace of dim night
Depart again: here, here will I remain
With worms that are thy chamber-maids; O, here
10 Will I set up my everlasting rest,
And shake the yoke of inauspicious stars
From this world-wearied flesh. Eyes, look your last!
Arms, take your last embrace! and, lips, O you
The doors of breath, seal with a righteous kiss
15 A dateless bargain to engrossing death!
Come, bitter conduct, come, unsavoury guide!
Thou desperate pilot, now at once run on

The dashing rocks thy sea-sick weary bark!
Here's to my love!

{Drinks}

20 O true apothecary!
Thy drugs are quick. Thus with a kiss I die.

Explore how Shakespeare presents Romeo as a character who is passionate in *Romeo and Juliet*.

Write about:

- *how Shakespeare presents Romeo in this speech.*
- *how Shakespeare presents Romeo in the play as a whole.*

[30 Marks] (AO1 = 12; AO2 = 12; AO3 = 6) + AO4 = Spelling and Grammar [4 marks]

(50 Minutes Total = 40 Minutes Writing + 10 Minutes Reading Extract / Making Notes / Planning)

(600 Words Maximum per Essay = 15 Words per Minute)

Shakespeare presents Romeo as a character who is passionate in this speech. As Romeo looks upon his wife Juliet he asks a rhetorical question, "Ah, dear Juliet, / Why art thou yet so fair?" There is a clear contrast here between Juliet's appearance of beauty and the death that surrounds her. Romeo declares his undying commitment to Juliet as he states, "...here, here will I remain" and Shakespeare uses fearful images which convey the finality of death, "With worms that are thy chamber-maids;". Romeo now sets his intention to escape his cruel fate and to leave his life and body "And shake the yoke of inauspicious stars/ From this world-wearied flesh". He passionately exclaims, "Eyes, look your last! / Arms, take your last embrace!" and as the soliloquy develops and just before he "{Drinks}" the poison he declares, "Here's to my love!" Shakespeare combines the use of emphatic statements, exclamatory remarks and imperative commands in Romeo's soliloquy to express the sense of immediate urgency in Romeo's actions. Shakespeare combines the themes of love and death in this extract and throughout the play which have an apparent contradictory duality yet for Romeo his suicide is a passionate act of love in order to join his wife, Juliet. Romeo is even appreciative of the immediate impact of the poison, thanking the apothecary for his fatal merchandise, "O true apothecary! /Thy drugs are quick.". His final words illustrate his passionate feelings of love for Juliet, "Thus with a kiss I die." Through the precision demonstrated by Shakespeare in this speech and the hyperbolic language and forceful phrasing used by Romeo, we can discern the sheer force of Romeo's will and the strength of his intention in this soliloquy.

Shakespeare presents this soliloquy in iambic pentameter and adds dramatic tension and power through his metaphorical use of the themes of love and death. There is an increasing sense of dramatic tension prior to this extract, which takes place in the final scene of the play. Romeo is a pivotal character in the play and his suicide is both a dramatic and structurally significant moment in the play. Romeo's passionate nature as presented in this extract and culminating in his death, endears him to the audience.

Shakespeare presents Romeo as a character who is passionate throughout the play. For example, when the play begins, Romeo is in love with Rosaline and Romeo's infatuation with her stands in obvious contrast to his later love for Juliet. Whilst Romeo's abandoning of Rosaline for Juliet could be viewed as fickle and reckless it provides a clear comparison through which the audience can discern the seriousness of Romeo and Juliet's love and marriage. Shakespeare's widespread use of the duality of light and dark imagery throughout the play also reflects this theme of light as being symbolic of natural, young love. The duality of light and dark is presented by Shakespeare in Act 1, Scene 1 when Romeo, infatuated with Rosaline, declares "O brawling love, O loving hate, / Feather of lead, bright smoke, cold fire, sick health," and shortly before his suicide when he views Juliet as a light in the surrounding darkness as she lies apparently dead in the Capulet tomb, stating that her "...beauty makes/ This vault a feasting presence full of light." Shakespeare therefore clearly presents Romeo as a character who is passionate. However, when Romeo murders Tybalt in Act 3 Scene 1 and declares "O, I am fortune's fool!" the audience is later left to reflect on whether it is fate or passion that led to the lovers' deaths at the end of the play.

(600 words)

AUTHOR'S NOTE

This book will provide you with 12 crystal clear and accurate examples of 'A' star grade (Grade 9) AQA GCSE English Literature Paper 1 Romeo and Juliet answers from the Shakespeare section of the new syllabus and enables students to achieve the same grade in their upcoming examinations.

I teach both GCSE and A level English and Psychology and I am a qualified and experienced teacher and tutor of over 17 years standing. I teach, write and provide independent tuition in central and west London.

The resources in this book WILL help you to get an A star (Grade 9) in your AQA GCSE English Literature examinations, as they have done and will continue to do so, for my students.

Best wishes,

Joseph

ABOUT THE AUTHOR

I graduated from the Universities of Liverpool and Leeds and I obtained first class honours in my teacher training.

I have taught and provided private tuition for over 17 years up to university level. I also write academic resources for the Times Educational Supplement.

My tuition students, and now, my readers, have been fortunate enough to attain places to study at Oxford, Cambridge and Imperial College, London and other Russell Group Universities. The students have done very well in their examinations. I hope and know that my English Literature books can enable you to take the next step on your academic journey.

Printed in Great Britain
by Amazon

43245543R00037